YOUR KNOWLEDGE HAS VALUE

- We will publish your bachelor's and master's thesis, essays and papers

- Your own eBook and book - sold worldwide in all relevant shops

- Earn money with each sale

Upload your text at www.GRIN.com
and publish for free

Bibliographic information published by the German National Library:

The German National Library lists this publication in the National Bibliography; detailed bibliographic data are available on the Internet at http://dnb.dnb.de .

Imprint:

Copyright © 2015 GRIN Verlag, Open Publishing GmbH
Print and binding: Books on Demand GmbH, Norderstedt Germany
ISBN: 978-3-668-09132-0

This book at GRIN:

http://www.grin.com/en/e-book/310165/design-and-implementation-of-a-model-to-predict-the-success-of-the-bank

Salma Bibi, Adeela Batool, Fatima Mustafa

Design and Implementation of a Model to Predict the Success of the Bank Telemarketing

GRIN Publishing

GRIN - Your knowledge has value

Since its foundation in 1998, GRIN has specialized in publishing academic texts by students, college teachers and other academics as e-book and printed book. The website www.grin.com is an ideal platform for presenting term papers, final papers, scientific essays, dissertations and specialist books.

Visit us on the internet:

http://www.grin.com/

http://www.facebook.com/grincom

http://www.twitter.com/grin_com

CERTIFICATE

It is certified that the contents and form of thesis entitled **"Design And Implementation Of A Model That Predicts The Success Of Bank Telemarketing** " submitted by **Adeela Batool, Fatima Mustafa, Salma Bibi** have been found satisfactory for the requirement of the degree.

DEDICATION

To Allah the Almighty

&

To our Parents and Faculty

ACKNOWLEDGEMENTS

We are deeply thankful to our supervisors Ms. Rabail Shafique Satti and Ms. Sidra Ejaz for helping us throughout the course in accomplishing our final project. Their guidance, support and motivation enabled us in achieving the objectives of the project.

The authors are not native speakers of English. Please excuse any linguistic mistakes.

Table of Contents

Table of Contents 4

INTRODUCTION 6

1.1 ID3 Algorithm: 6

1.2 Objective: 7

1.3 Problem Statement: 8

1.4 Project Scope: 8

1.5 Report Organization: 8

LITERATURE REVIEW 10

SYSTEM DESIGN 12

3.1 Introduction: 12

3.2 Proposed Model Design: 12

    3.2.1 Logical Design (Flow Diagram): 13

    3.2.2 Use Case Diagram: 14

    3.2.3 Time Sequence Diagram 15

    3.2.4 Structural diagram: 16

IMPLEMENTATION 17

4.1 System Development Requirements: 17

    4.1.1 Software Requirements: 17

    4.1.2 Hardware Requirements: 17

4.2 Data Set Description: 17

    4.2.1 Attribute Description: 18

4.3 Decision Tree: 20

    4.3.1 Decision Tree Algorithm: 20

    4.3.2 Pseudo code: 21

    4.3.3 Root node: 22

    4.3.4 For further nodes (i.e. Internal and Leaf nodes): 22

RESULTS 23

CONCLUSION 27

FUTURE WORK 27

REFERENCES 28

ABSTRACT

Targeting customer is a major task of bank telemarketing to send their service to customers. Now banks are using a number of data mining techniques to predict the success rate. Decision Tree is successful data mining technique for predicting bank telemarketing success. Decision Tree is a well known classifier and is simple and easy to apply. Performance of decision trees can be improved with appropriate attribute selection. In this research, ID3 decision tree technique of data mining is applied on widely used benchmark data set. The main focus of this research was on designing and implementation of a model that predicts the success of bank telemarketing using decision tree technique of data mining.

Decision Tree is powerful techniques of DM which is used for the Success of Bank Telemarketing. The proposed system makes bank telemarketing more efficient. And the proposed system's Database will be flexible to incorporate new changes at the same time keeping data secure. It is a need of bank telemarketing to gain the confidence of their profitable customers in order to retain their loyalty. Service providers need to closely track the trend in their industry so they can position themselves for a competitive edge in the future. Evolving technology, Rejection, Fake Calls is also a big challenge in telemarketing. The proposed system can be implemented in any bank telemarketing company to aid their decision making process and predict the customers who are more likely to involve with the new upcoming product in the market.

5

INTRODUCTION

Telemarketing is a marketing process in which bank or any other businesses can promote their services or product to the customers through telemarketing service, E-mail service. It is also called direct marketing because businesses are directly connected with their customers. Telemarketing is more useful when the customers are located in hard-to-reach places, so companies use telemarketing to advertise or provide their services information to customer. Telemarketing is most often used as part of an overall marketing program to tie together advertising and personal selling efforts

In banks, a large amount of data recorded about their customers. This recorded data can be used to keep direct relationship and create connection with the customers in order to target them individually for banking offers. The selected customer are directly connected through remote communication channels like cellular phone, mail, e-mail and any other source of communication. This is known as direct marketing. Direct marketing is a main source of many insurance companies and banks for connecting with their customers. Now many banks have adopted classification and prediction techniques of data mining to understand the customer behavior by predicting the customer data before offering services. By using data mining techniques, banks can send services or information to only those customers which are classified by the data.

Decision Tree popular is a power tool for prediction and classification. Decision Tree is admirable tools for helping out to select between some courses of action. It is a tree-shaped diagram that is used to find out a course of action or illustrate a statistical probability. Every branch of the decision tree shows possible decision or occurrence. Decision tree structure shows that how one option directs to the next. The use of branches shows that each option is mutually exclusive. Decision tree represents rules. Rules can be stated so one can understand them or can be directly used in a database language like SQL so that records falling in a particular group may be retrieved. Decision tree is a classifier that is in form of tree structure in which each node is a leaf node (point to value of the target attribute or class) or a decision node (points to some test to be done on a single attribute with one branch and sub-tree for each possible outcome).

1.1 ID3 Algorithm:

The proposed system used ID3 algorithm. ID3 algorithms stand for Iterative Dichotomiser 3.It is presented by J. Ross Quinlan in 1986. ID3 is a no incremental algorithm, which means it derives its classes from a fixed set of training instances. It builds the shortest and fastest tree. In ID3, prediction rules are created from training set. It is very efficient algorithm in terms of processing time as it searches the whole dataset to create tree and can handle continuous attribute. It is used to calculate logistic calculations. In ID3 algorithm, one attribute is tested at a time for making a decision. ID3 is a supervised algorithm.

A statistical property called information gain that is used for attribute selection. The attribute with the highest information gain is selected from training data set. In order to define information gain we must calculate the entropy measures, the amount of information in an attribute.

ID3 uses dataset to generate decision tree in top-down fashion. The tree is constructed in ID3 in two phases. One is tree building and second is pruning. ID3 use gain approach to determine suitable property for each node generated in decision tree.ID3 starts from set of objects. One property is tested based on maximizing information gain and minimizing entropy at each node of the tree, and then results are used to split objects. This process is continuous recursively until objects belongs to same category. Then it becomes the leaf node of the decision tree

Formulas and procedure of ID3 algorithm is following:

- Select that attribute which has highest information gain

- Let p_i be the probability that an arbitrary tuple in D belongs to class C_i, estimated by $|C_{i,D}|/|D|$

- Expected information (entropy)
$$Info(D) = -\sum_{i=1}^{m} p_i \log_2(p_i)$$

- Information needed
$$Info_A(D) = \sum_{j=1}^{v} \frac{|D_j|}{|D|} \times Info(D_j)$$

- Information gained through branching on attribute A
$$Gain(A) = Info(D) - Info_A(D)$$

1.2 Objective:

The main focus of this research was on designing and implementation of a model that predicts the success of bank telemarketing using decision tree technique of data mining. Decision Tree is

7

powerful techniques of DM which is used for the Success of Bank Telemarketing. The proposed system makes bank telemarketing more efficient. And the proposed system's Database will be flexible to incorporate new changes at the same time keeping data secure.

1.3 Problem Statement:

It is a need of bank telemarketing to gain the confidence of their profitable customers in order to retain their loyalty. Service providers need to closely track the trend in their industry so they can position themselves for a competitive edge in the future. Evolving technology, Rejection, Fake Calls is also a big challenge in telemarketing.

1.4 Project Scope:

The proposed system can be implemented in any bank telemarketing company to aid their decision making process and predict the customers who are more likely to involve with the new upcoming product in the market.

1.5 Report Organization:

The report is organized into four chapters.

Chapter 2 is of literature review, a literature survey for this research is explained there. Different research paper represents the importance of using ID3 in extracting rules using decision tree are discussed in this chapter. The dataset used in research is widely benchmark data set which is then used for predicting the success of bank telemarketing.

Chapter 3 describes the logical design of research project. Use case and UML diagrams are drawn to represent the flow of project. Design makes the work simpler and easy to understand. Flowchart represents whole activity of project in a manner that's easy to understand. Structural Diagram represents whole view of system. Time sequence represents whole activity with respect to time event. State machine is used to represent change from one state to another.

Chapter 4 is about the implementation of project of this research. It represents the tools used for implementation. Software and Hardware required for the project are mentioned. Dataset used is described. Decision tree algorithm used in project is explained.

Chapter 5 describes the results.

Chapter 6 is conclusion of whole research and future work we can do. The best part of research element are explored along with the mode of implementation is presented in this chapter of thesis.

LITERATURE REVIEW

There are number of research work available for predicting the success of bank telemarketing using different techniques.

Feature Selection for Prediction of Bank Telemarketing was proposed by Chakarin Vajiramedhin et al [1]. Telemarketing is an impressive technique for marketing both for direct and the predictive. This technique is mainly used by the banks for long term deposits. This is done through phone calls which make the customers exasperated. A useful approach called data mining approach is used for predicting and solving problems such problems. This approach may fail when there is a huge amount of data having many features. This paper focuses on the ways how to minimize the input features and then apply the predictive techniques to produce more accurate results. Results are measured by comparing to expected results with the actual results. In this way the performance of the system can be analyzed.

This paper introduces the concept of using enhanced ID3 algorithm DID3 for decision making especially in bank sector. This concept was proposed by Ahmed Bahgat El Seddawy et al [2] which was rarely discussed before. Decision support system a system is such a system that contains and manages information. This information could be individual data or data from external data sources. Its purpose is to do a deep understanding of data and then use it for decision making. Success of any decision system can measure by the quality of data entered, understanding level, availability, timely presentation. This can be used as a repository for internal and external data. Tools, models and user interface give enough information required for decision making Strategy making, implementation, and critical decision-making and evaluation are its key factors. The system uses classification technique by DID3algorithm which allows the top level management for decision making in any uncertain environment.

Sergio Moro et al presented a Data-Driven Approach to Predict the Success of Bank Telemarketing [3]. Data of calculate form the year of 2009 to 2014 which shows the results of crises in terms of finance. Data contain about 150 features which includes product name, job type, campaign, client name etc. A semi-automatic technique for feature selection was applied on this dataset which minimize the dataset into 22 features. Comparison of various algorithms were carried out which includes neural networks, decision trees etc. Results were examined through evaluation phase. Neural Networks produced the excellent results that classify clients. Two more models were included in neural network which highlights some key attributes such as call

10

direction, bank agent experience etc. Such models and results were considered very important for the mangers.

Data mining approach for bank telemarketing using Rimer package and R tool was proposed by Paulo Cortez et al [4] .Mostly in banks direct telemarketing campaigns are carried out in order to examine client's interests. The paper examines the trends of the market and extracts a valuable knowledge. This was done through data mining techniques using Rimer and R tool. It uses ROC and Lift curve Analysis methods for analysis for which neural basiyan and vector machine algorithms was undertaken. Results show that Support vector machine produces the excellent results and a useful knowledge was extracted. This extracted knowledge then becomes the basis for future pattern analysis. Now the mangers and the telemarketing companies are putting more emphasize on predicting techniques for pattern evaluation instead of tradition analysis techniques.

Bank Direct Marketing Based on Neural Network was proposed by Hany. A. Elsalamony, et al [5] .Bank telemarketing is all about customers. Classification of such a huge amount of data is impossible to handle for any human. This give rises to the development of some interesting patterns and procedures for decision making process. Data mining is a great approach to solve such problem both in terms of performance and accuracy. This paper analyses different models for classification based on previous and new researches. A new algorithm called as Multilayer Perception Neural Network (MLPNN) with combining features of C5.0. This research aims to measure the performance of this model on real world data. It analyzed how to increase the efficiency by highlighting those factors that have an effect on measuring success. Performance of the system was measures using these measures such as classification correctness, understanding, and specificity.

Rupali Bhardwaj et al [6] presented ID3 algorithm in 1975. ID3 is a supervised algorithm builds decision tree from examples of fixed sets, than the resulting tree is used to classify the future samples. This algorithm is used for producing good classification results. It takes a given set of attributes and then inductive methods are used. Appropriate results if ID3 leads them to be used in intelligent systems as well. This paper uses ID3 algorithm implementations training set data of approximately two weeks for making decisions. Java language was used for predicting results. Results were concluded inform of a decision tree and rules generation. Thos shows that ID3 works well for any dataset having discrete values.

11

SYSTEM DESIGN

3.1 Introduction:

Design of specific system gives outlook or appearance of that system. It shows the functionality of the system, its performance and it also show data storing and manipulation property in order to accomplish its task.

Design has to exhibit following qualities:

- Should be Easy to understand and simple one.

- Must explain working of system completely and clearly.

- It can cover user needs

- Can be mold it in to any shape and

- Should be Reliable

It also shows particular method, procedures or set of procedures that has been followed for developing any project, particular to the branch of knowledge.

3.2 Proposed Model Design:

The design of the research is based on flow diagram, use case diagrams, structural diagram, time sequence diagram.

3.2.1 Logical Design (Flow Diagram):

The logical Diagram of system includes the flow diagram or block diagrams which are graphical or symbolic representation of system work.

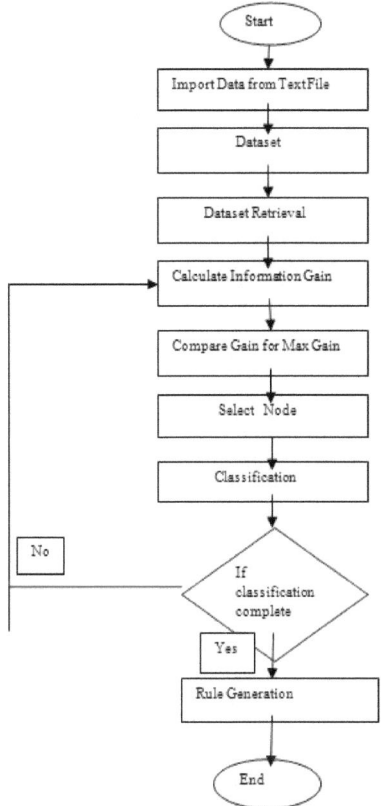

Figure 1 Flow Diagram of Complete System

3.2.2 Use Case Diagram:

Use case describes a relation between user and system. Use case diagram help analysis to discover the requirements of the target system from the user's perspective.

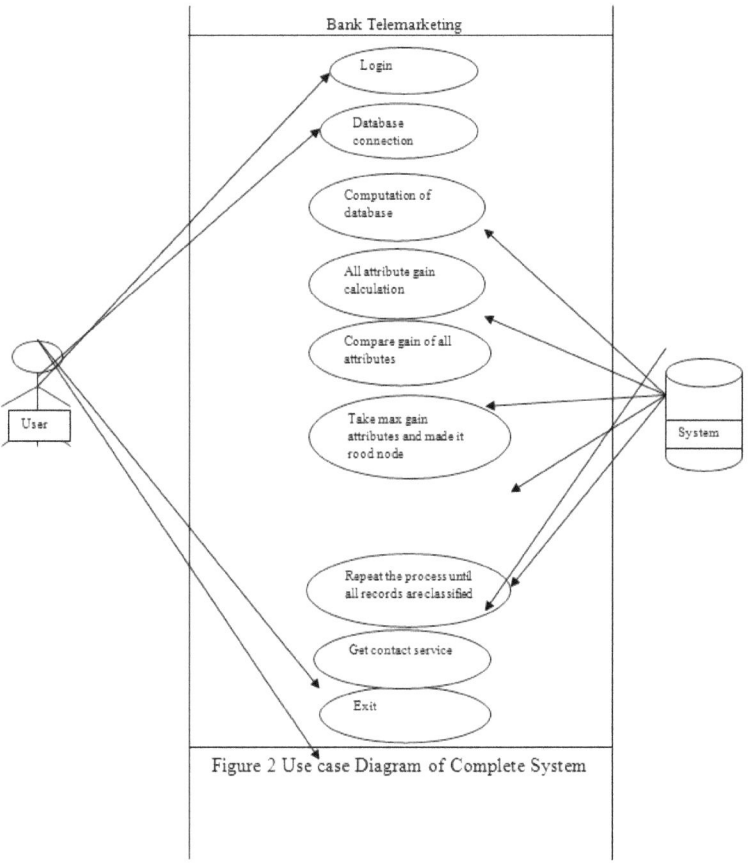

Figure 2 Use case Diagram of Complete System

3.2.3 Time Sequence Diagram

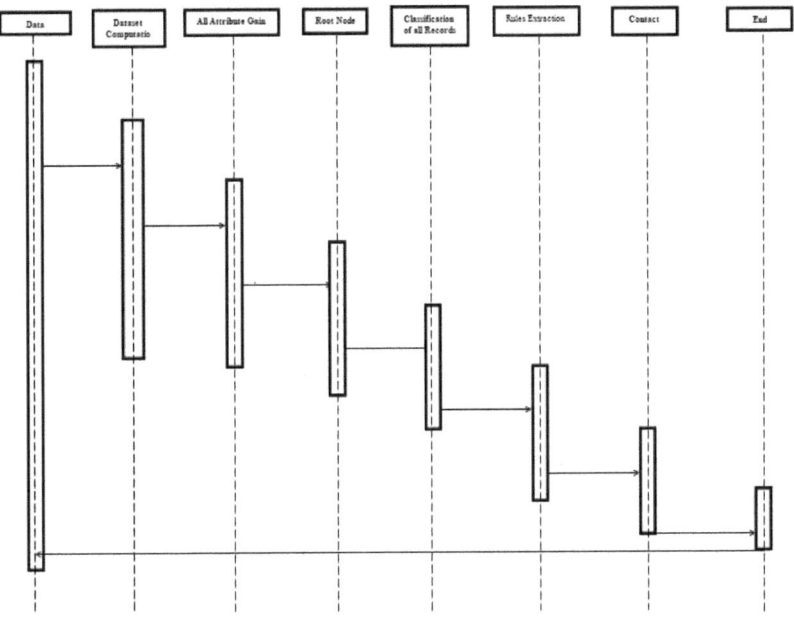

3.2.4 Structural diagram:

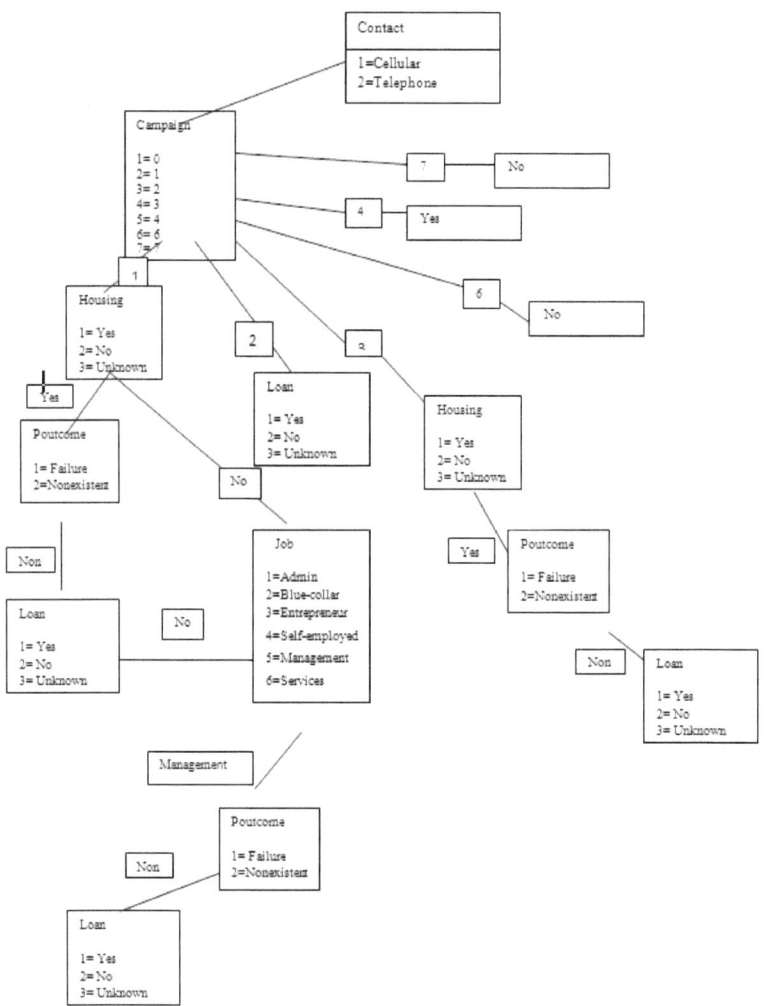

IMPLEMENTATION

This chapter contains the required information about the tool and technique used for the implementation of the proposed system.

4.1 System Development Requirements:

4.1.1 Software Requirements:

Minimum requirements to run this software are:

- Environment for system development is Microsoft Visual Studio C# 2010.

4.1.2 Hardware Requirements:

Minimum hardware requirements to run this software are:

- 2 GB (Minimum 256MB) RAM
- Dual Core or Higher Processor
- Minimum 40 GB of Hard Disk

4.2 Data Set Description:

Datasets from UCI database is used. This database contains 7 attributes which have been extracted from a set of 15. Attributes are:

Table of Attributes Definition:

No	Name	Type
1	Age	Numeric
2	job	Categorical
3	Housing	Categorical
4	Loan	Categorical

5	Campaign	Numeric
6	Pout come	Categorical
7	Contact	Categorical

4.2.1 Attribute Description:

1.   Age (3 values):

Age refers to duration during which a person uses services. Age is measured in years, months, weeks, days. Unit used in this research for age is "year".

- <=55
- 25-55
- >25

2.   Job (7 values):

Job refers to the duties that can be done in a specific duration. It can be done by human being either male or female.

- Admin
- Blue-collar
- Entrepreneur
- Self-employed
- Management
- Services
- Technician

3.   Housing (3 values):

It is a service which is provided by banks to their customers. It has two possible values

- Yes

- No

- Unknown

4.   **Loan (3 values):**

It is a service which is provided by banks to their customers. It has two possible values

- Yes

- No

- Unknown

5.   **Contact (2 values):**

It is a communication medium between bank and customers. It can be through cellular phones or telephone.

- Cellular
- Telephone

6.   **Campaign (7 values):**

It is categories into following:

- 0
- 1
- 2
- 3
- 4
- 6
- 7

7.   **Poutcome (2 values):**

It is the Outcome of the previous marketing campaign.

- Failure
- Nonexistent

4.3 Decision Tree:

It is a popular and powerful tool for prediction and classification. Decision Tree is an admirable tool for helping out to select between some actions. It is tree-shaped diagram which is used to find out a possible action or demonstrate a statistical probability. Each branch of the decision tree shows possible occurrence or decision. Decision tree configuration shows that how one option directs to the next. The use of branches shows that each option is mutually exclusive. Decision tree represents rules.

Entropy:

Entropy is a measure of how "mixed up" an attribute is. It is sometimes equated to the purity or impurity of a variable. Decision tree uses entropy to calculate the homogeneity of example. If the example is completely homogeneous the entropy is zero and if the example is an equally divided it has entropy of one [19].

Information Gain:

In general terms, the expected information gain is the change in information entropy from a prior state to a state that takes some information. The information gain is based on the decrease in entropy after a dataset is split on an attribute. Constructing a decision tree is all about finding attribute that returns the highest information gain (i.e., the most homogeneous branches)[19].

Formulas for Entropy and Gain:

$$Entropy\ (y) = \sum_{j=1}^{n} (|y_j|/|y|)*\mathbf{log}\ (|y_j|/|y|)$$

$$Entropy\ (j|y) = (|y_j|/|y|)*\mathbf{log}\ (|y_j|/|y|)$$

$$Gain\ (y, j) = Entropy\ (y - Entropy\ (j|y))$$

4.3.1 Decision Tree Algorithm:

function Decision_tree()

int no.of nodes;

for int 0<i<no.of nodes

calculate gain g(n) of all nodes;

g(n) = -((x / (x + y)) * Math.Log((x / (x + y)), 2)) - ((y / (x + y)) * Math.Log((y / (x + y)), 2));

create an array arrb;

arrb[] = g(n);

max g(n);

store max g(n) in dataset;

compare max g(n) with all nodes;

extract root node rn;

end for

eliminate root node

compare remaining g(n)

foreach

calculate all remaining nodes r(n)

generate rules

end foreach

end **Function** *Decision_tree()*

4.3.2 Pseudo code:

The general algorithm in pseudo code for making decision trees is:

- Ensure for base cases

- For each attribute *b*

- Calculate information gain from splitting on *b*

- Let *b_best* be the attribute with the highest information gain

- Make decision *node* that splits on *b_best*

- Recurse on the sub attributes obtained by splitting on b_*best*, and add those nodes as child *nodes*

Description:

Calculate information gain and gain ratio for each attribute by using its frequencies and its sub class's frequencies. Store all attribute's gain in array of size 30, compare them and find maximum gain by arr.Max(). Extract root node that is attribute having highest gain. Repeat this until all records or tuples for all attributes are classified. Rules are generated according to classified records. Now end decision tree.

4.3.3 Root node:

Root node extracted by using 60 rows of dataset is that will give us two outputs cellular and telephone where people using telephonic services will Get No. And cellular will further processed and classified.

4.3.4 For further nodes (i.e. Internal and Leaf nodes):

From 2 sub attributes of Contact, tree is drawn and classified. 12 records are of No means people will not do telemarketing, 14 records are of Yes means people will do telemarketing and 19 records are of no-effect means people will have no effect on telemarketing. From Contact next node is Campaign which is further processed and classified. Further housing, loan, and job, p-outcome which is further processed and is classified.

RESULTS

The Bank telemarketing system has following results.

Log in

Import data file

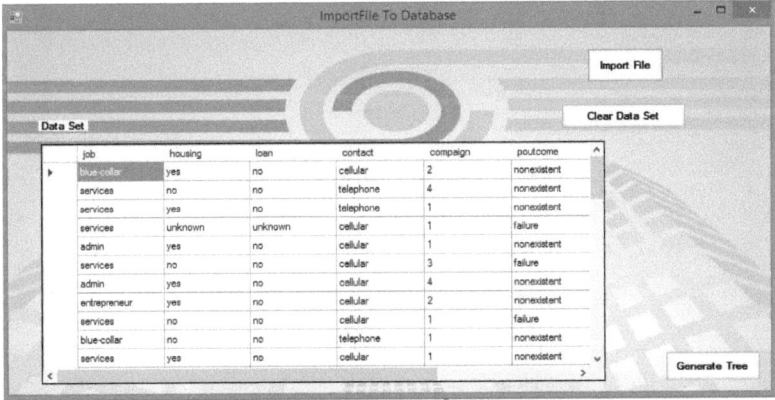

Generate Tree

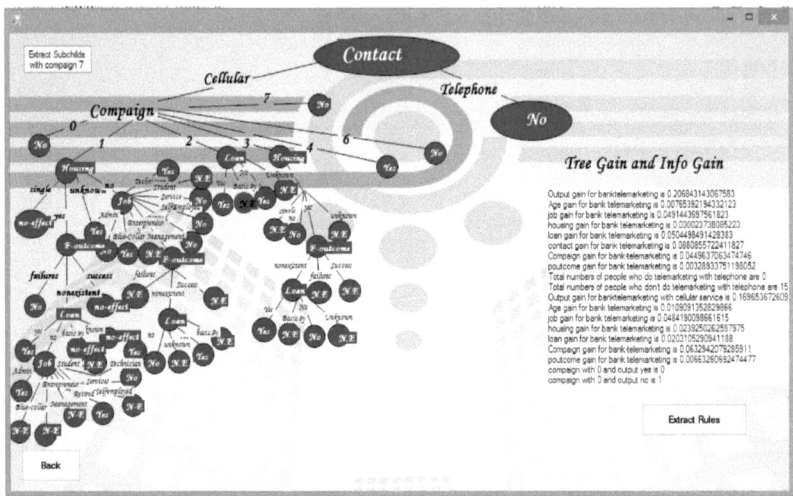

Rules Generation

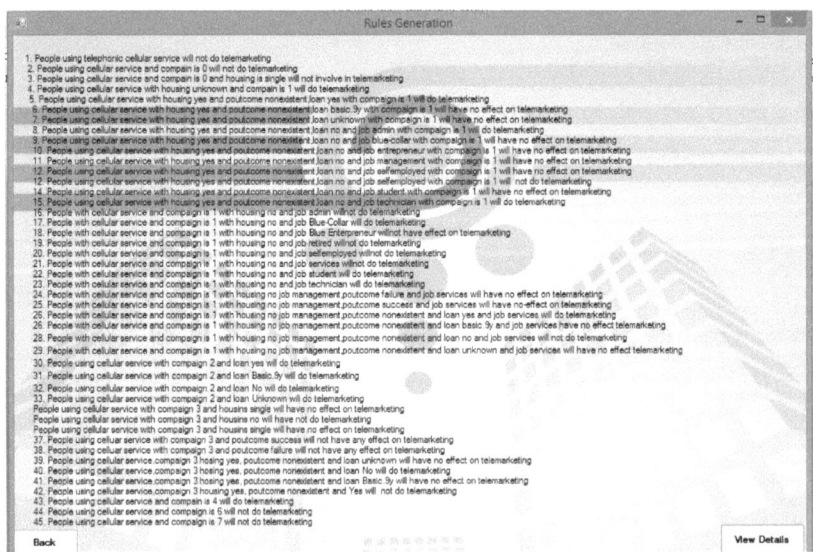

Services

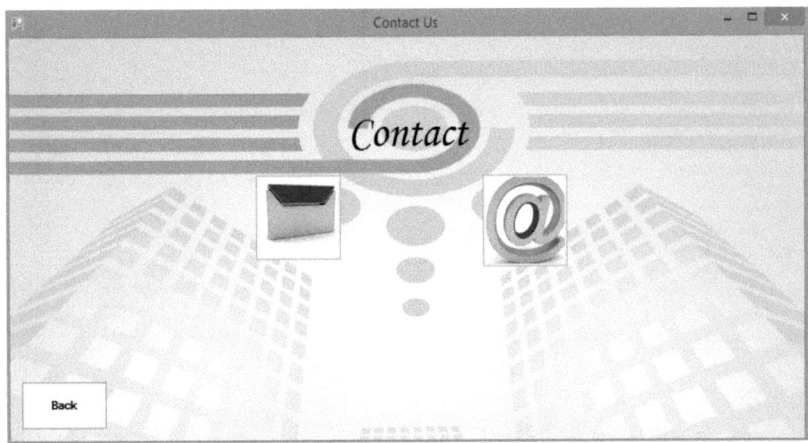

E-mail

Short Message Service

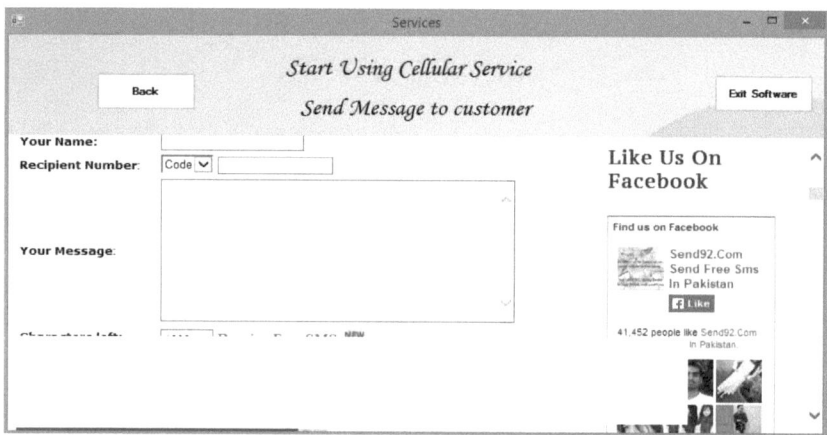

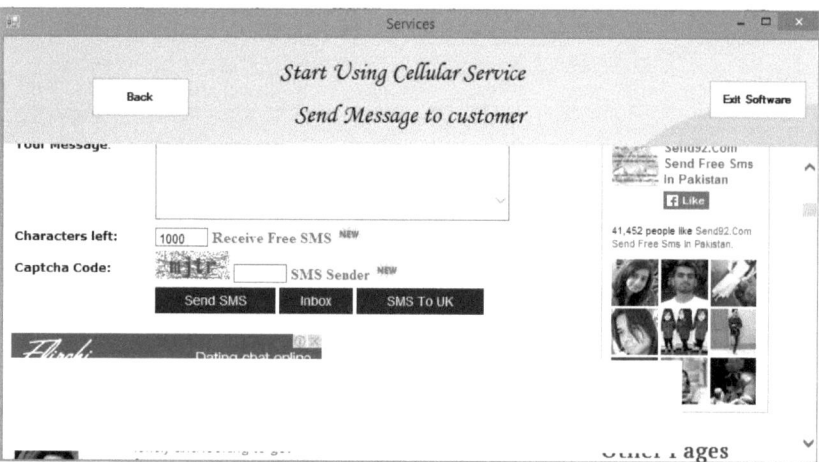

CONCLUSION

We have used decision tree technique of data mining for predicting the success of bank telemarketing. Datasets from UCI database has been used for training as well as for testing. From UCI database 7 attributes has been used. 60 records are used as training data for decision tree. The proposed system predicts the bank telemarketing among given dataset from database. Rules are generated according to which banks can do telemarketing. ID3 algorithm is used in this research.

FUTURE WORK

Decision tree is a significant technique used for predicting the success of bank telemarketing. The proposed system predicts success of bank telemarketing using 7 attributes using a generic dataset, UCI dataset. In future, we can do it for more than 7 attributes. Web based model based on rules can be generated. Moreover, these implemented rules can be used to generate offers to the valuable customers We can also predict success of bank telemarketing with artificial neural networks, genetic algorithm and support vector machine technique of data mining.

REFERENCES

[1] Chakarin Vajiramedhin (2011, June 5). Feature Selection for Prediction of Bank Telemarketing (2nd ed.) Available: http://www.Informationbuilders.com/decisio-support-system-dss

[2] Ahmed Bahgat El Seddawy.(2010, March 12). Enhanced ID3 algorithm DID3 for decision making (8th ed.) Available: http://www.cs.sfu.ca/~oschuite/king.pdf

[3] Sergio Moro.(2011,Sept 22). A data-driven approach to predict the success of bank telemarketing (10thed.) Available: http://www.igcseict..info/theory/7_2/expert/pdf

[4] Paulo Cortez et al (2011, June 2005). Data mining approach for bank telemarketing using Rimer package and R tool (10thed.) Available:www.ssrn.com/link/world-bank.html

[5] Hany. A. Elsalamony, et al 2013, Sept 22). Bank Direct Marketing Based on Neural Network was proposed (10thed.) Available: http://www.igcseict..info/theory/7_2/expert/pdf

[6] Rupali Bhardwaj et al (2011, Sept 22). Implementation of ID3 Algorithm(10thed.) Available: http://www.igcseict../expert/pdf

[7] Theodorou, G.(2014,Aug,17). A data-driven approach to predict the success of bank telemarketing (10thed.) Available: http://www.igcseict..info/theory/7_2/expert/pdf

[8] Sergio,Moro. Predicting customer purchases in an online retail business, A data mining Approach (5thed.)Available: http://www.ftc.gov/sites/default/files/documents/reports/federal-trade-commission-report-congress/dnciareportappenda.pdf

[9] Gerali, A., Neri, S., Sessa, L. and Signoretti, F. (2010). Credit and Banking in a DSGE Model of the Euro Area. In "Journal of Money, Credit and Banking" (Wiley), Vol. 42(1), pp. 107–141. Available:http:// bru-unide.iscte.pt/RePEc/pdfs/13-06.pdf

[10] Silva, A., Cortez, P., Santos, M., Gomes, L. and Neves, J. (2008). Rating Organ Failure via Adverse Events using Data Mining in the Intensive Care Unit. In "Artificial Intelligence in Medicine", Elsevier, (Vol. 43) Available: http://www.igcseict..info/theory/7_2/expert/pdf